# Plant-Based Diabetes Cookbook for Beginners

*1000 Days Vegan, Gluten-Free, Oil-Free Recipes for the Newly Diagnosed / A 4-Week Meal Plan to Manage Type 2 Diabetes and Prediabetes*

Cristy Heiler

# CONTENTS

ELEPHANTS, RHINOS, bison, wildebeest, and horses are among the animals on display. These powerful animals may be paving the way for a healthy eating plan, as they all adhere to a vegetarian diet. People with diabetes, like everyone else, should eat foods that are beneficial to their health. However, food selection is critical in controlling blood sugar levels in people with diabetes.

According to research, eating a plant-based diet has been shown to have significant benefits for people with diabetes, including lower blood sugar levels, lower lipid levels, and lower body weight. And for those of you who cringe at the thought of adopting a plant-based eating plan, you might reconsider your position after reading this.

Many ways are eating more plant-based foods benefits people with diabetes:

- Better blood sugar management.
- Improved heart health.
- Weight loss.
- Lower lipid levels.

When it comes to plant-based diets, it's not a case of all or nothing. Making small changes to achieve big results, such as keeping blood sugar levels within normal range and improving overall health, is something I believe in wholeheartedly. The transition to a plant-based eating plan can begin with as little as increasing the number of vegetables served at one meal per day or "going vegetarian" for one meal per week.

You may have heard of the campaign known as Meatless Monday, which encourages people to replace animal protein with plant protein on Mondays every week. The following days of the week, Tempeh Thursday and Salad Bowl Sunday, are good options if Mondays don't work for your schedule: Tempeh Thursday and Salad Bowl Sunday.

Small steps toward a plant-based diet can have a significant impact on your overall health and well-being. The reason for this is as follows: Increased fiber is associated with improved blood glucose control:

According to the Institute of Medicine, the typical American Diet falls far short of the daily recommended dietary fiber intake, which varies from 21 grams to 38 grams depending on age and gender. When following a plant-based eating plan, it is easier to consume foods that are high in fiber - whole grain foods such as whole wheat, fruits and vegetables, and even plant-based proteins, which include legumes (such as lentils and chickpeas), beans (such as black beans and lima beans), soy (such as edamame, tofu and tempeh), nuts and seeds (such as peanuts, peanut butter), pistachios, walnuts, and even though some of these foods contain carbohydrates, the fiber helps to slow down the absorption of carbohydrates, which helps to prevent spikes in blood sugar levels. A plant-based eating plan will provide you with an average of 40 grams of fiber per day, which is more than the amount recommended by the Institutes of Medicine for adults.

Perhaps you've thought about going vegan in the past, or perhaps your spouse has been encouraging you to consider switching to a vegetarian diet, or perhaps the thought of even removing meat from your Diet is unthinkable; whatever your position on vegetarianism, this article may be able to provide you with a little perspective shift on the subject.

There are many misconceptions about vegetarians, including that they are unhealthy or pale, that they are deficient in certain nutrients that can only be obtained through meat products, and that they are incapable of reproducing. This is far from the truth, as a well-balanced meal can provide all of the nutrition that can be found in a well-balanced diet containing animal products and all of the nutrition that can be found in a vegan diet.

We've already established that losing weight and making dietary changes can effectively prevent type 2 diabetes. The question is whether you really need to go to such lengths as adopting a vegan diet to see a positive effect on your blood sugar control or whether a diet low in saturated fat and high in fiber should be sufficient to achieve the desired results.

Diet for Diabetes Prevention

The National Institute of Health (United States) decided to investigate whether or not a plant-based diet is actually that beneficial. According to the findings of their study, which compared both a well-balanced vegan diet and an individualized diet (which included animal products), it is clear that the former was superior to the latter in terms of long-term weight loss achievement and better cholesterol control. In addition, those who followed a plant-based diet required less medication for blood sugar control in the long run. When the nutrient intake of the two groups was compared, the plant-based diet did not appear to be deficient in nutrients that are traditionally believed to be deficient in vegan diets.

For those of you who are skeptical or do not believe that you will be able to keep up with the pace of change, consider the following: Be open to the possibility that surveys of young women who had tried either a vegetarian or calorie-restricted diet had found that they had a mean duration of adherence to the vegetarian diet of at least 2 years, compared to only 4 months for calorie-restricted diets, you may be surprised to find out that This could be because those who make the switch to a vegan diet are more committed to the change than those who do not because the transition is so abrupt. Ultimately, it all comes down to how committed a person is to their lifestyle modification and how much control they want over the progression of their disease.

# PART ONE: PLANT BASED AND DIABETES

To keep things short and simple, a Plant-Based Diet is essentially a type of dietary program that encourages you to follow a diet routine solely focused on consuming edible products derived entirely from plants. Therefore, it is also known as a plant-based diet.

While the program's core is very similar to that of a Vegan Diet, you should be aware that some differences vary depending on which variation of the Plant-Based Diet you choose to adhere to. Because of this variety, it is one of the most accessible programs available today, as you can select the one that best suits your needs.

Consider, for example, those who adhere to the Plant-Based Diet in its purest Vegan form. They strictly limit themselves to plant-based foods and products only. In contrast, some vegetarians choose a more lenient approach that allows for consuming dairy products in moderation.

The important thing to remember is that, regardless of which variation you choose to follow, you will need to avoid all processed and refined foods for them to be compatible with the Plant-Based Program.

So, allow me to provide you with a breakdown of the most frequently encountered variations.

## PLANT-BASED DIET VARIATIONS

**Ovo-Lacto Vegetarianism:** This diet version allows you to have dairy and eggs alongside fruits and vegetables.

**Ovo-Vegetarianism:** This version will allow you to eat eggs alongside fruits and vegetables but not milk.

**Fruitarianism:** This version is a form of a vegan diet that mostly surrounds the consumption of fruits. If you have diabetes, then this might be the perfect one for you!

**Vegetarianism:** Vegetarians mostly prefer to stick to fruits and vegetables, but they also have the liberty to sometimes indulge themselves in eggs and dairy if they choose.

**Veganism:** This is regarded as the most common, well-known, and followed form of plant-based Diet today. This version will encourage you to consume more legumes, fruits, grains, vegetables, seeds, nuts, etc., while letting go of anything even remotely derived from animals.

**Semi-Vegetarianism:** This program isn't that strict compared to the core vegetarian program, as it only asks you to be a full vegetarian most of the time while also having the option to opt for meat from time to time.

**Pescatarian:** This is very similar to the Semi-Vegetarian diet program; however, it allows you to have dairy, eggs, shellfish, and fish, but no red meat such as beef, poultry, pork, etc.

**Macrobiotic Diet:** This variation mostly focuses on the consumption of whole-grain, miso, sea vegetables, vegetables, naturally processed foods, and so on. It is possible to follow through with this program without opting for either seafood or other types of animal products.

Again, I cannot stress this enough. Regardless of which variation you choose, a Plant-Based Diet will always ask you to let go of any kind of Processed and Refined food from Your Diet.

## WHAT TO EAT

L et me walk you through the foods you will mostly be eating/avoiding since you now have a basic understanding of the Plant-based Diet.

Keep in mind that some of these Ingredients: might change depending on the form of the Plant-Based Diet that you are following, but the core will still remain the same.

That being said, here's what you should keep in mind:

**Ingredients: to consume more**

**Starchy vegetables**

- Potatoes
- Legumes
- Lentils
- Beans
- Whole corn

- Root vegetables
- Quinoa

## Non-Starchy Vegetables

- Leafy greens
- Broccoli
- Eggplant
- Tomatoes
- Broccoli
- Spaghetti Squash
- Olives
- Okra
- Avocado
- Onions

And more

## Whole Grains

- Brown rice
- Oats
- Whole Wheat

## Beverages

- Unsweetened plant milk
- Decaffeinated coffee
- Tea
- Water

## Omega 3 Sources

- Flax Seeds
- Chia Seeds

## Ingredients: to consume less/occasionally

## Nuts

- Almonds
- Cashews
- Peanuts
- Walnuts

## Seeds

- Dried Fruit
- Coconut
- Avocado
- Sesame
- Pumpkin
- Sunflower

**Added Sweetener**

- Maple Syrup
- Fruit Juice concentrates
- Natural sugar

**Refined Protein**

- Refined Soy
- Wheat Protein

**Others**

- Tofu
- Wheat
- Gluten Protein
- Soy Protein Isolate

## HEALTH BENEFITS OF PLANT-BASED DIET

L etting your body go through a dietary shift and allowing it to focus on meals made of fresh fruits and vegetables bears a myriad of health benefits with it.

Below are just some of the crucial ones that you ought to know:

**Faster Workout Recovery**

A plant-Based Diet boosts your body in antioxidants, vitamins, potassium, and other essential minerals while decreasing the intake of anti-inflammatory compounds. This altogether helps your body to recover from fatigue faster.

**Healthier Stomach**

Consuming too much meat, dairy, and processed food might often lead to heartburn and indigestion. A Plant-Based Diet will help you to avoid those.

## Improved Digestion

A plant-based diet will give you a very significant boost in the consumption of fiber. These additional fibers will help you to improve your digestion and prevent a bloaty stomach.

## Enhanced Immune System

The nutrients, antioxidants, and other essential minerals coming from plant-based meals will significantly help boost your immune system's strength.

## Improved Skin And Complexion

Dairy and sugar are two ingredients that are significantly believed to be triggered by food linked to acne and several different skin diseases. However, once you let them go and move to whole foods, your skin will slowly start to rejuvenate and heal itself in the long run.

## Boosted Energy

Once the body starts getting its energy from healthy plant-based food full of nutrients instead of harmful carbohydrates and sugar, the body will eventually begin to stay more energized. This aids the body in getting a constant supply of energy throughout the day instead of having sudden spikes of blood sugar levels.

## Protects from diseases

Lastly, the Plant-Based Diet will help you improve your resistance against several deadly conditions such as:

- Chronic Inflammation
- Diabetes
- Heart Diseases
- Alzheimer's
- Dementia
- Stroke
- Cancer

Just to name a few.

According to Frank Qian, MPH, a current medical student at the University of Chicago and a coauthor of the study, previous summary studies of observational studies and randomized controlled trials have shown that substituting plant-based sources of protein or fat for those derived from animal sources is associated with improved heart and metabolic health, among other benefits. According to a presentation given at the 2019 American Heart Association meeting, increasing your intake of high-quality plant-based foods lowers your risk of dying prematurely from heart disease and other causes. Fruits, vegetables, whole grains, and legumes are some of the foods on this list.

Plant-based diets provide the body with hundreds of beneficial compounds that interact with one another through countless pathways to influence weight homeostasis, glucose-insulin response (which has been linked to a variety of health conditions in the past), inflammation and oxidative stress (which have been linked to various health conditions in the past), gut microbiome composition and function, according to Qian. "All of these pathways are likely to play a role in the beneficial association that we observed," he continues.

The effects of plant-based diets on weight control suggest Dr. Sun could be responsible for a portion of the risk reduction. In previous observational and interventional studies, "the majority of the foods that make up a plant-based diet have been shown to mediate weight loss or to prevent long-term weight gain," says Qian.

Because the researchers were interested in measuring the benefits of a plant-based diet rather than the benefits of weight loss, they made sure that BMI was considered in the statistical analyses. In the study, Sun and colleagues "basically removed the benefits of weight control from the estimated reduction in diabetes risk associated with eating plant-based diets." As a result, the 23 percent risk reduction may be an underestimate, and the risk reduction may be even greater if a person also loses weight, according to the researcher.

According to Golubic, "It's important to remember that someone can eat a completely plant-based diet that is high in sugar and refined grains such as bread and pasta, and that is clearly not beneficial." According to him, eating foods like this actually increases the risk of developing diabetes and other diseases.

A ccording to Golubic, the majority of the diets included in this study did not completely eliminate meat. His research participants frequently included a few servings of meat and fish in their diets. Still, their diets were primarily plant-based, according to him. Several studies have linked red meat and processed meat to an increased risk of diabetes and other chronic health conditions, according to a review published in February 2014 in Nutrients. According to Golubic, eating less red meat and processed meat would be beneficial from a health standpoint.

According to Qian, even though research, including studies cited in an August 2017 article in Nutrients, has shown that plant-based diets are extremely safe to follow and may provide various health benefits, you should always consult with a healthcare professional before making any dietary changes. , This is because the extremely strict plant

According to Golubic, taking small steps toward a more plant-based diet can be beneficial. He offers a few suggestions on how to begin making your Diet more environmentally friendly:

Consume a greater variety of vegetables. Golubic believes that, even though it appears obvious, the United States is failing in this area. Even though it has been shown that eating vegetables and fruit can help protect us from a variety of diseases, only 10 to 12 percent of people consume three servings of vegetables and two servings of fruit per day, according to Dr. Friedman.

Fruit can be served as a dessert. However, according to Golubic, people substitute a piece of fruit for cake or a cookie in many cultures and diets such as the Mediterranean diet.

Increase the amount of fiber in your diet. Golubic recommends substituting legumes for animal protein, such as chickpeas, hummus, or beans, high in fiber and low in fat. According to him, this will shift the proportion of animal foods to plant foods in the Diet.

## HOW FAT AND CARBOHYDRATES CAUSE DIABETES

Whenever we eat something, the starches in the food are broken down into glucose in our digestive system, which then circulates as blood glucose ("blood sugar") and is taken up by our muscles, where it is either stored (as glycogen) or burned and used for energy.

Insulin acts as a "key1" to open the door to the muscle cells, allowing glucose to enter the cells. Without insulin, glucose would remain in the bloodstream, gradually increasing in concentration until it reached a state known as hyperglycemia or high blood sugar. Type 1 diabetes occurs when the cells in the pancreas that produce insulin are damaged and therefore unable to produce insulin. As a result, insulin injections are required to transport glucose from the bloodstream into the muscles.

Type 2 diabetes, on the other hand, is characterized by the presence of normal insulin. Still, the insulin cannot 'unlock' the muscle cells, preventing the sugar from entering the muscle cells and instead of remaining in the blood, resulting in dangerously high levels of blood sugar. So why is it that insulin cannot unlock the muscle cell and allow the sugar to enter? Intramyocellular lipids, which are tiny droplets of fat found inside our muscle cells and block the pathway into the muscle cells, prevent glucose from entering.

Fat in the bloodstream accumulates inside muscle cells, resulting in toxic fatty breakdown products and free radicals that interfere with the insulin signaling pathway.

No matter how much insulin we have in our blood, it is not sufficient to open the glucose gates, resulting in a buildup of glucose levels in the blood. And this may occur within three hours. In addition, studies have shown that a single serving of fat can cause insulin resistance, inhibiting glucose uptake in the bloodstream after only 160 minutes.

It wasn't until the development of MRI techniques that it was possible to see exactly what was happening inside people's muscles as fat was infused into their bloodstream that the mechanism by which fat causes insulin resistance was discovered. We discovered that increasing fat levels in the blood causes insulin resistance by inhibiting glucose transport into the muscles in this manner. Conversely, when the level of fat in people's blood is reduced, insulin resistance in the blood returns to normal.

The fact that a high-fat ketogenic style diet is unhealthy (because it causes insulin resistance) is one of the reasons for this. With a decrease in the amount of fat in our Diet, insulin functions better and better.

After examining the relationship between diet and diabetes rates in various countries, we have discovered that as carbohydrate intake decreases and fat intake increases, the number of diabetics rapidly increases. In addition, we have observed that when people relocate to countries where the standard 'Western' style diet predominates and adopt this Diet, their rates of type 2 diabetes rise above the national average.

According to additional research, consuming even one serving of meat per week significantly increases the risk of developing diabetes in the long run. 8,000 adult Seventh-Day Adventists participated in a study that examined the relationship between meat consumption and the occurrence of diabetes. All of the participants were healthy and had no diabetes at the time of the study's inception. According to the findings of this long-term study, those who followed a 'low-meat diet for 17 years increased their risk of developing type 2 diabetes by an astounding 74 percent compared to those who followed a meat-free diet for the same period.

However, even after accounting for these factors, meat consumption continued to be a significant risk factor for developing type 2 diabetes.

The results of another study published in 2018 revealed a remarkable discovery that corroborated the findings of previous research. According to the researchers, insulin resistance was assessed in young healthy adults who had family members who had diabetes. It was discovered that those who tested positive for the drug had microscopic drops of fat in their muscle cells. The presence of this fat interfered with the cells' ability to respond appropriately to insulin. Thus, even though their bodies produced enough insulin, the fat stored within their cells prevented the proper reactions.

Studies have shown that carbohydrates can help to lower the risk of developing diabetes. Among patients with type 2 diabetes, an experiment was conducted. The participants were given either a high-protein diet or a high-carbohydrate diet. A high-carbohydrate group was instructed to consume more bread, cereal, pasta, and starchy vegetables; a high-protein group was instructed to consume more fish, chicken, eggs, low-fat milk and cheese. Nuts were encouraged to consume more nuts. The experiment was carried out over eight weeks, and the participants' fat intake was maintained at a constant level of 30%. Both groups lost the same amount of weight. Still, only the carbohydrate group saw improved diabetes (i.e., their blood sugar control was better).

Low-carbohydrate diets have also been shown to increase the risk of type 2 diabetes - one study found a 37% increase in the risk of developing the disease. Interestingly, several studies have also found that low-carbohydrate diets based on animal sources are associated with an increased risk of developing diabetes. In contrast, low-carbohydrate plant-based diets are associated with reduced risk.

Several studies have also found a link between low-carbohydrate diets and increased mortality from all causes, including cardiovascular disease and cancer.

## GENERAL TREATMENT FOR TYPE 2 DIABETES

Drugs or a change in one's way of life are used as treatments. Unfortunately, drugs have many side effects. Still, lifestyle changes are extremely effective in treating diabetes. For example, it has been shown repeatedly that a whole food plant-based diet that is free of dairy and meat and low in saturated animal fat is an extremely effective treatment for Crohn's disease. People with diabetes, high cholesterol, and heart disease can reverse their conditions with a whole food plant-based diet, and they may even be able to stop taking their medications.

Studies have revealed that some medications can lower blood sugar levels while also increasing the risk of heart attack and stroke and causing other negative side effects in some patients.

In its statement, the Academy of Nutrition and Dietetics, the world's largest professional organization of dieticians, says that vegetarian and vegan diets are appropriate for all stages of life, from infancy to adulthood, and may have benefits in the prevention and treatment of diabetes, obesity, and ischemic heart disease.

Indeed, dozens of studies have now demonstrated the effectiveness of a plant-based diet in preventing and treating diabetes.

The use of a plant-based diet to control diabetes has the added benefit of lowering the risk of heart disease, cancer, obesity, stroke, and hypertension due to the reduced risk of diabetes. Studies on treating diabetes with a high-carbohydrate, low-fat diet have been published since the 1950s. However, in 2003, the American Diabetes Association (ADA) published the first major randomized clinical trial on diabetic patients treated purely with a plant-based (vegan) diet, comparing it to a conventional diet based on the 2003 ADA guidelines.

A total of 99 participants, ranging in age from 27 to 82 years, were randomly assigned to either a low-fat vegan diet or the ADA diet. Their progress was monitored for 22 weeks. The recommended vegan Diet consisted primarily of vegetables, fruits, grains, and legumes. It provided approximately 10% of total energy from fat, 15% from protein, and 75% from carbohydrates. The recommended vegan Diet was composed primarily of vegetables, fruits, grains, and legumes.

Participants in the vegan group were instructed to refrain from consuming animal products or consuming added fats and to prioritize foods with a low glycemic index, such as beans and green vegetables. After completing the trial, 43 percent (21 of 49) of vegan group participants and 26 percent (13 of 50) of ADA group participants reduced their intake of diabetes medications. Except for those who switched medications, hemoglobin Ale fell 1.23 points in the vegan group, compared to 0.38 points in the ADA group, after adjusting for medication changes. The vegan group lost 6.5 kg of body weight, while the ADA group lost 3.1 kg of body weight.

Furthermore, LDL cholesterol decreased by 21.2 percent in the vegan group and 10.7 percent in the ADA group. lowering the likelihood of having a heart attack

## HOW CAN PLANT-BASED DIET HELP REVERSE DIABETES

According to research, plant-based diets have been shown to improve blood sugar control in various ways. For example, vegetarian and vegan diets tend to be low in saturated fat, which, as we previously discussed, can cause lipotoxicity by impairing insulin signaling in liver and muscle cells and decreasing glucose uptake from the bloodstream.

However, the story does not end there.

Plant-based diets are high in fiber, antioxidants, and magnesium, all of which have improved insulin sensitivity in their own right in separate studies.

The gut bacteria of vegans produce significantly less trimethylamine N-oxide (TMAO). This compound has been linked to insulin resistance as well as a higher risk of atherosclerosis.

In addition, plant-based diets contain significantly lower levels of other dietary elements associated with insulin resistance, such as advanced glycation end products, nitrosamines, and heme iron, than animal-based diets. Many of these dietary elements also increase the risk of heart disease, which, as previously stated, is already higher in diabetics due to their increased blood glucose levels.

Diabetics need to monitor their blood sugar and blood pressure closely after switching to a plant-based diet, especially if they are taking medications for these conditions. Close monitoring and anticipation of low blood sugar are essential, as medications may need to be adjusted or discontinued altogether to avoid blood sugar levels becoming dangerously low (hypoglycemia).

Many organizations are now recognizing the advantages of adopting a plant-based diet to prevent and treat diabetes and other diseases of blood sugar.

Many large healthcare organizations, such as Kaiser Permanente, are promoting plant-based diets for all of their patients and employees because it is a cost-effective, low-risk method of treating a wide range of chronic illnesses at the same time. It is viewed as an important tool in addressing the rising cost of health care. Plant-based diets have been shown to improve metabolic control in people with diabetes, according to the American Diabetes Association's Clinical Practice Guidelines published in 2010.

However, as documented in the 2017 documentary What The Health, the American Dietetic Association (ADA) receives significant financial support from meat and dairy companies and pharmaceutical companies. As a result, don't expect the ADA to advocate for the elimination of animal products or adopting a plant-based diet for treatment or reversal of disease as long as this situation persists.

## RESEARCH ON PLANT-BASED DIET FOR DIABETES

According to new research, following a plant-based diet is likely to lower the risk of developing type 2 diabetes in adults. In addition, according to the study's findings, diets that are low in sugar, starch, and refined grains are more beneficial in preventing this chronic illness in people of all ages and, regardless of their body mass index, are more beneficial (BMI).

An article published on Monday in the medical journal JAMA Internal Medicine elaborated on the importance of consuming a diet rich in fruits, nuts, vegetables, legumes, and whole grains to maintain a healthy weight.

Dr. Qi Sun, an assistant professor in the Department of Nutrition at Harvard T.H. Chan School of Public Health in Boston, said in a statement that the study's findings showed that eating plant-based diets was associated with a 23 percent reduction in diabetes risk on average. In addition, we found that people who followed a healthy version of the plant-based diet, emphasizing the intake of fresh fruits, vegetables, whole grains, nuts, and legumes while minimizing the intake of sugar-sweetened beverages and refined carbohydrates, had a further 30 percent lower risk of developing type 2 diabetes." According to the researcher, "I would characterize these risk reductions as quite significant."

According to the World Health Organization (WHO), the number of people diagnosed with type 2 diabetes is increasing at an alarming rate worldwide. According to the World Health Organization, the number of people suffering from this chronic illness has increased from 108 million in 1980 to 422 million in 2014.

According to the Centers for Disease Control and Prevention (CDC), more than 30 million people in the United States, or nearly one in every ten people, have diabetes, with type 2 diabetes accounting for approximately 95 percent of cases, according to the CDC.

Specifically, the data from nine previous studies, which included 23,544 cases of type 2 diabetes, were analyzed by the research team for this study. Each of the previously published studies attempted to establish a connection between this chronic disease and a plant-based diet.

The researchers discovered a plant-based eating habit after their new study can lower the risk of type 2 diabetes in all age groups regardless of their BMI, even though obesity is thought to increase the risk of developing this disease.

Although the research did not specifically state whether a completely vegetarian diet is more beneficial than a plant-based diet that includes animal products, the senior study author stated that even a plant-based diet that includes animal products can be beneficial.

A senior study author explained that "there are many types of diets that can be regarded as plant-based diets, ranging from the strict vegan diet to vegetarian diets to diets that emphasize the intake of plant-based foods but do not completely exclude animal product intake." "There are many types of diets that can be regarded as plant-based diets," she said.

The Mediterranean diet and the DASH diet are predominantly plant-based eating patterns, so keep that in mind when planning your meals. Individuals who are currently following these diets, in my opinion, are on the right track," he continued.

However, the study has its own limitations, primarily because the dietary data collected for the study was based on people's self-reported eating habits, which raises the possibility of inaccurate and biased results. In addition, the study's researchers were unable to determine whether there is a coincidental relationship between a plant-based diet and the risk of developing type 2 diabetes. As a result, more research will be required to back up this claim.

# PART TWO: FOUR WEEKS

**Day 1**

Breakfast: Delicious Nut Porridge

Lunch: Portobello Mushroom Risotto

Dinner: Everyday Traditioanl Chili

**Day 2**

Breakfast: Vanilla And Flaxseed Meal

Lunch: Cilantro And Avocado Platter

Dinner: Delicious Garlic Toast

**Day 3**

Breakfast: Flaxseed Porridge

Lunch: Baby Potato Roast

Dinner: Lemon And Thyme Couscous

**Day 4**

Breakfast: Delicious Nut Porridge

Lunch: Portobello Mushroom Risotto

Dinner: Everyday Traditioanl Chili

**Day 5**

Breakfast: Vanilla And Flaxseed Meal

Lunch: Cilantro And Avocado Platter

Dinner: Delicious Garlic Toast

**Day 6**

Breakfast: Flaxseed Porridge

Lunch: Baby Potato Roast

Dinner: Lemon And Thyme Couscous

**Day 7**

Breakfast: Delicious Nut Porridge

Lunch: Portobello Mushroom Risotto

Dinner: Everyday Traditioanl Chili

**Day 1**

Breakfast: Pumpkin Steel Cuts

Lunch: Tasty Roasted Broccoli

Dinner: Sesame Cucumber Mix

**Day 2**

Breakfast: Savory Oatmeal Delight

Lunch: Sticky Mango Rice

Dinner: Cashew Mushroom Risotto

**Day 3**

Breakfast: Vanilla And Flaxseed Meal

Lunch: Fine Black Bean Soup

Dinner: Authentic Zucchini Boat

**Day 4**

Breakfast: Pumpkin Steel Cuts

Lunch: Tasty Roasted Broccoli

Dinner: Sesame Cucumber Mix

**Day 5**

Breakfast: Savory Oatmeal Delight

Lunch: Sticky Mango Rice

Dinner: Cashew Mushroom Risotto

**Day 6**

Breakfast: Vanilla And Flaxseed Meal

Lunch: Fine Black Bean Soup

Dinner: Authentic Zucchini Boat

**Day 7**

Breakfast: Pumpkin Steel Cuts

Lunch: Tasty Roasted Broccoli

Dinner: Sesame Cucumber Mix

**Day 1**

Breakfast: Almond And Spinach Glass

Lunch: Roasted Onion And Green Onion

Dinner: Meditternean Kale Dish

**Day 2**

Breakfast: Hungarian Breakfast Bowl

Lunch: Hearty Roasted Cauliflower

Dinner: Lemon And Thyme Couscous

**Day 3**

Breakfast: Easy Apple Porridge

Lunch: Garbanzo And Spianch Beans

Dinner: Hearty Kale Pasta

**Day 4**

Breakfast: Almond And Spinach Glass

Lunch: Roasted Onion And Green Onion

Dinner: Meditternean Kale Dish

**Day 5**

Breakfast: Hungarian Breakfast Bowl

Lunch: Hearty Roasted Cauliflower

Dinner: Lemon And Thyme Couscous

**Day 6**

Breakfast: Easy Apple Porridge

Lunch: Garbanzo And Spianch Beans

Dinner: Hearty Kale Pasta

**Day 7**

Breakfast: Almond And Spinach Glass

Lunch: Roasted Onion And Green Onion

Dinner: Meditternean Kale Dish

**Day 1**

Breakfast: Simple Apple Pie

Lunch: Tasty Tofu And Mushroom Soup

Dinner: Lemon And Thyme Couscous

**Day 2**

Breakfast: Tasty Vegetable Morning Hash

Lunch: Whole Wheat Penne With Summer Veggies

Dinner: Delicious Garlic Toast

**Day 3**

Breakfast: Hearty Walnut Porridge

Lunch: Mushroom Cream Soup

Dinner: Grilled Eggplant Steak

**Day 4**

Breakfast: Simple Apple Pie

Lunch: Tasty Tofu And Mushroom Soup

Dinner: Lemon And Thyme Couscous

**Day 5**

Breakfast: Tasty Vegetable Morning Hash

Lunch: Whole Wheat Penne With Summer Veggies

Dinner: Delicious Garlic Toast

**Day 6**

Breakfast: Hearty Walnut Porridge

Lunch: Mushroom Cream Soup

Dinner: Grilled Eggplant Steak

**Day 7**

Breakfast: Simple Apple Pie

Lunch: Tasty Tofu And Mushroom Soup

Dinner: Lemon And Thyme Couscous

# PART THREE: THE RECIPES

## PERFECT SMOKED PEACHES

Preparation Time: 10 minutes

Cooking Time: 20 minutes

Serve: 4

**Ingredients:**

- 6 fresh peaches

**Directions:**

1. Pre-heat your smoker to 200 degrees F
2. Transfer peaches directly onto your smoker and smoke for 30 minutes; the first 20 minutes should be skin side down while the final 10 should be skin side up
3. Remove from smoker and serve, enjoy!

**Nutritional Value (Amount Per Serving):**

- Calories: 117
- Fat: 28g
- Carbohydrates: 0.8g
- Protein: 3g
- Sugar: 0.2 g

Preparation Time: 10 minutes

Cooking Time: 20 minutes

Serve: 4

**Ingredients:**

- 5 apples
- ¼ cup sugar
- 1 tablespoon cornstarch
- Flour as needed
- 1 refrigerated pie crust
- ¼ cup peach preserve

**Directions:**

1. Pre-heat your smoker to 275 degrees F
2. Take a medium-sized bowl and add apples, sugar, cornstarch and stir well until combined thoroughly
3. Transfer to one side
4. Dust a work surface with flour and roll out your pie crust
5. Transfer pie crust into pie pan (not greasing)
6. Spread preserve on bottom of pan and top with apple slices
7. Transfer into smoker and smoke for 30-40 minutes
8. Serve and enjoy!

**Nutritional Value (Amount Per Serving):**

- Calories: 236
- Fat: 9g
- Carbohydrates: 39g
- Protein: 2g
- Sugar: 5 g

Preparation Time: 10 minutes

Cooking Time: 60-90 minutes

Serve: 4

**Ingredients:**

- 1 eggplant halved lengthwise
- 1 tablespoon of olive oil
- 2 and a ½ teaspoon of salt
- 2 and a ½ tablespoon of tahini
- Juice of 1 lemon
- 1 garlic clove minced
- 2 tablespoons of chopped fresh parsley
- Pita chips

**Directions:**

1. Pre-heat your smoker to 200 degrees Fahrenheit
2. Rub eggplant halves with olive oil and sprinkle 2 teaspoons of salt
3. Place the halves o smoker rack and smoker for about 1 and a ½ hours
4. Remove and peel off the skin; discard it
5. Transfer eggplant flesh to a food processor
6. Add tahini, garlic, lemon juice, 1/ a teaspoon of salt and blend well
7. Transfer to a storage
8. Stir in parsley and serve with pita chips
9. Enjoy!

**Nutritional Value (Amount Per Serving):**

- Calories: 334
- Fat: 25g
- Carbohydrates: 28g
- Protein: 1g
- Sugar: 4 g

Preparation Time: 5 minutes

Cooking Time: 2 minutes

Serve: 4

**Ingredients:**

- 2 cups stock, chicken
- ½ tablespoon turmeric
- 1 bay leaf
- 1 cup rice, long grain
- 1 tablespoon coconut butter, unsalted

**Directions:**

1. Rinse long-grain rice until water runs clear
2. Add rice to Instant Pot except for butter, stir
3. Stir
4. Lock lid and cook on HIGH pressure for 3 minutes
5. Naturally, release the pressure over 10 minutes
6. Remove lid and add butter
7. Fluff up and serve

**Nutritional Value (Amount Per Serving):**

- Calories: 301
- Fat: 4g
- Carbohydrates:  58g
- Protein: 9g
- Sugar: 5 g

Preparation Time: 5 minutes

Cooking Time: 22 minutes

Serve: 4

**Ingredients**

- 2 cups brown rice
- 2 and ½ cups of water

**Directions:**

1. Add rice to the Pot
2. Add water and lock up the lid
3. Cook on HIGH pressure for 22 minutes
4. Release the pressure naturally and enjoy your favorite dish!

**Nutritional Value (Amount Per Serving):**

- Calories: 180
- Fat: 2g
- Carbohydrates:  25g
- Protein: 4g
- Sugar: 3 g

Preparation Time: 10 minutes

Cooking Time: No Cook Time

Serve: 4

**Ingredients:**

- 2 cups fresh spinach, chopped
- 1 and ½ cups of almond milk
- ½ cup of coconut water
- 3 cups fresh pineapple, cubed
- 2 tablespoons unsweetened coconut flakes

**Directions:**

1. Add the listed Ingredients: to your blender/food processor and blend until smooth
2. Serve chilled and enjoy!

**Nutritional Value (Amount Per Serving):**

- Calories: 200
- Fat: 4g
- Carbohydrates: 40g
- Protein: 3.6g
- Sugar: 3 g

Preparation Time: 10 minutes

Cooking Time: No Cook Time

Serve: 4

**Ingredients:**

- 1 ripe pear, cored and chopped
- 2 cups kale, chopped
- ¼ cup mint leaves
- 1 cup of water
- 1 cup apple juice

**Directions:**

1. Add the listed Ingredients: to your blender/food processor and blend until smooth
2. Serve chilled and enjoy!

**Nutritional Value (Amount Per Serving):**

- Calories: 135
- Fat: 0.3g
- Carbohydrates: 32g
- Protein: 3g
- Sugar: 4 g

Preparation Time: 10 minutes

Cooking Time: No Cook Time

Serve: 2

**Ingredients:**

- 1 ripe peach, chopped
- 1 banana, diced
- 1 and ¼ ounces spinach
- 1 teaspoon agave syrup
- 1 cup of coconut water

**Directions:**

1. Add the listed Ingredients: to your blender/food processor and blend until smooth
2. Serve chilled and enjoy!

**Nutrition Values (Amount Per Serving):**

- Calories: 120
- Fat: 0.7g
- Carbohydrates: 28g
- Protein: 2g
- Sugar: 6 g

Preparation Time: 10 minutes

Cooking Time: No-Cook time

Serve: 2

**Ingredients:**

- 1 cup unsweetened almond milk
- 1 tablespoon almond butter
- 1 scoop protein powder
- ½ banana
- 1 teaspoon cinnamon, ground
- 3 carrots, shredded

**Directions:**

1. Add the listed Ingredients: to your blender/food processor and blend until smooth
2. Serve chilled and enjoy!

**Nutrition Values (Amount Per Serving):**

- Calories: 400
- Fat: 14g
- Carbohydrates: 42g
- Protein: 28g
- Sugar: 4 g

Preparation Time: 10 minutes

Cooking Time: No Cook Time

Serve: 2

**Ingredients:**

- 2 cups spinach
- ½ banana, diced
- 1 tablespoon protein powder
- ½ teaspoon cinnamon
- ½ cup yogurt
- 1 and ½ cups unsweetened almond milk

**Directions:**

1. Add the listed Ingredients: to your blender/food processor and blend until smooth
2. Serve chilled and enjoy!

**Nutrition Values (Amount Per Serving):**

- Calories: 396
- Fat: 21g
- Carbohydrates: 40g
- Protein: 20g
- Sugar: 5 g

# BREAKFAST

## HUNGARIAN BREAKFAST BOWL

Preparation Time: 10 minutes

Cooking Time: 5-10 minutes

Serve: 2

**Ingredients:**

- 1 tablespoon chia seeds
- 1 tablespoon ground flaxseed
- 1/3 cup coconut cream
- ½ cup water
- 1 teaspoon vanilla extract
- 1 tablespoon coconut butter

**Directions:**

1. Add chia seeds, coconut cream, flaxseed, water and vanilla to a small pot
2. Stir and let it sit for 5 minutes
3. Add butter and place pot over low heat
4. Keep stirring as butter melts
5. Once the porridge is hot/not boiling, pour it into a bowl
6. Enjoy!
7. Add a few berries or a dash of cream for extra flavor

**Nutritional Value (Amount Per Serving):**

- Calories: 410
- Fat: 38g
- Carbohydrates: 10g
- Protein: 6g
- Sugar: 6 g

Preparation Time: 10 minutes

Cooking Time: 15 minutes

Serve: 4

**Ingredients:**

- 1 cup cashew nuts, raw and unsalted
- 1 cup pecan, halved
- 2 tablespoons stevia
- 4 teaspoons coconut oil, melted
- 2 cups water

**Directions:**

1. Chop the nuts in a food processor and form a smooth paste
2. Add water, oil, stevia to nuts paste and transfer the mix to a saucepan
3. Stir cook for 5 minutes on high heat
4. Lower heat to low and simmer for 10 minutes
5. Serve warm and enjoy!

**Nutritional Value (Amount Per Serving):**

- Calories: 260
- Fat: 22g
- Carbohydrates: 12g
- Protein: 6g
- Sugar: 6 g

Preparation Time: 10 minutes

Cooking Time: 5 minutes

Serve: 2

**Ingredients:**

- 1 large apple, peeled, cored and grated
- 1 cup unsweetened almond milk
- 1 and a ½ tablespoon of sunflower seeds
- 1/8 cup of fresh blueberries
- ¼ teaspoon of fresh vanilla bean extract

**Directions:**

1. Take a large pan and add sunflower seeds, vanilla extract, almond milk, apples, and stir
2. Place it over medium-low heat
3. Cook for 5 minutes, making sure to keep the mixture stirring
4. Transfer to a serving bowl
5. Serve and enjoy!

**Nutritional Value (Amount Per Serving):**

- Calories: 123
- Fat: 1.3g
- Carbohydrates:23g
- Protein: 4g
- Sugar: 4 g

Preparation Time: 10 minutes

Cooking Time: 5-10 minutes

Serve: 4

**Ingredients:**

- 1 cup almond milk
- ¼ cup coconut flour
- 1 teaspoon cinnamon
- ¼ cup flaxseed, ground
- 1 teaspoon vanilla extract
- 10 drops stevia
- Pinch of salt

**Directions:**

1. Heat almond milk in a saucepan over low heat, whisk in coconut flour, salt, cinnamon, flaxseed
2. Stir well; once it bubbles, adds vanilla and stevia
3. Remove heat and add some garnish and berries as a topping
4. Enjoy!

**Nutritional Value (Amount Per Serving):**

- Calories: 405
- Fat: 134g
- Carbohydrates: 12g
- Protein: 10g
- Sugar: 2 g

Preparation Time: 10 minutes

Cooking Time: 5-10 minutes

Serve: 2

**Ingredients:**

- 3 tablespoons water
- 2 tablespoons flaxseed
- Pinch of salt
- 1 and ½ tablespoons coconut oil
- ½ scoop vanilla vegan powder
- ¼ teaspoon baking powder

**Directions:**

1. Take a bowl and mix in flaxseeds and water, mix in the oil
2. Mix in baking powder, protein powder, and salt
3. Stir well
4. Add wet Ingredients: to dry Ingredients: and mix properly
5. Take a non-stick pan and place it over medium heat
6. Scoop batter into your pan and cook for 5 minutes, flip and cook for 2 minutes more
7. Repeat until all batter has been used up
8. Enjoy!

**Nutritional Value (Amount Per Serving):**

- Calories: 309
- Fat: 20g
- Carbohydrates:5g
- Protein: 13g
- Sugar: 1 g

Preparation Time: 10 minutes

Cooking Time: 5-10 minutes

Serve: 2

**Ingredients:**

- 1 cup almond milk
- 1 teaspoon cinnamon
- ¼ cup coconut flour
- ¼ cup ground flaxseed
- 10 drops stevia
- 1 teaspoon vanilla extract
- Pinch of salt
- 1 ounce's coconut, shaved for garnish
- 2 ounces blueberries for garnish
- 2 tablespoons almond butter, garnish
- 2 tablespoons pumpkin seeds, garnish

**Directions:**

1. Take a saucepan and place it over low heat
2. Whisk in coconut flour, salt, cinnamon, flaxseed, and stir
3. Add stevia, vanilla, and heat until bubbling
4. Remove from heat
5. Mix in remaining Ingredients: and stir
6. Garnish with blueberries, pumpkin seeds or almond and serve
7. Enjoy!

**Nutritional Value (Amount Per Serving):**

- Calories: 400
- Fat: 34g
- Carbohydrates: 12g
- Protein: 10g
- Sugar: 2 g

Preparation Time: 10 minutes

Cooking Time: 23 minutes

Serve: 4

**Ingredients:**

- 1 tablespoon sage leaves, chopped
- 1 bell pepper, diced
- 3 garlic cloves, minced
- 1 onion, diced
- 3 tablespoon olive oil
- 3 red potatoes, diced
- 15 ounces black beans, canned
- 1 tablespoon parsley, chopped
- 2 cups swiss chard, chopped
- Salt and pepper

**Directions:**

1. Take a skillet and place it over medium heat, add oil and let it heat up
2. Add potato, garlic and onion cook them for about 20 minutes
3. Add Swiss Chard, beans, cook for 3 minutes
4. Season well with salt and pepper, serve with parsley
5. Enjoy!

**Nutritional Value (Amount Per Serving):**

- Calories: 270
- Fat: 11g
- Carbohydrates: 40g
- Protein: 9g
- Sugar: 4 g

Preparation Time: 10 minutes

Cooking Time: 15 minutes

Serve: 4

**Ingredients:**

- 1 and ½ cups of water
- ½ cup coconut milk, unsweetened
- 1 cup Teff, whole grain
- ½ teaspoon cardamom, ground
- 1 teaspoon salt, fine
- ¼ cup walnuts, chopped
- 1 tablespoon maple syrup, pure

**Directions:**

1. Take a large bowl and place it over medium heat, add coconut oil and water, bring to a boil and stir in your Teff
2. Add cardamom, lower heat and simmer for 20 minutes
3. Mix in walnuts, maple syrup and serve
4. Enjoy!

**Nutritional Value (Amount Per Serving):**

- Calories: 312
- Fat: 18g
- Carbohydrates:35g
- Protein: 7g
- Sugar: 4 g

Preparation Time: 10 minutes

Cooking Time: 20-25 minutes

Serve: 4

**Ingredients:**

- 3 cups of water
- 1 cup steel-cut oats
- ½ cup pumpkin puree, canned
- ¼ cup pumpkin seeds
- 2 tablespoons maple syrup
- Pinch of salt

**Directions:**

1. Take a large saucepan and place it over high heat, add water and let it boil
2. Add oats, stir and lower heat, simmer for 20-25 minutes
3. Stir in pumpkin puree and keep cooking for 3-5 minutes
4. Stir in pumpkin seeds, maple syrup and season with salt
5. Serve and enjoy!

**Nutritional Value (Amount Per Serving):**

- Calories: 121
- Fat: 5g
- Carbohydrates: 5g
- Protein: 4g
- Sugar: 2 g

Preparation Time: 2 minutes

Cooking Time: 25 minutes

Serve: 2

**Ingredients:**

- 2 and ½ cups vegetable broth
- 2 and ½ cups unsweetened almond milk
- ½ cup steel cut oats
- 1 tablespoon farro
- ½ cup almonds, slivered
- ¼ cup nutritional yeast
- 2 cups old fashioned rolled oats
- ½ teaspoon salt

**Directions:**

1. Take a large saucepan and place it over medium heat, add broth and milk, bring to a boil
2. Add oats, farro, almonds, yeast and cook over medium-high heat for 20 minutes
3. Add rolled oats and cook for 5 minutes more
4. Stir in salt, top with some berries
5. Serve and enjoy!

**Nutritional Value (Amount Per Serving):**

- Calories: 208
- Fat: 14g
- Carbohydrates: 22g
- Protein: 14g
- Sugar: 3 g

# LUNCH

## ROASTED ONIONS AND GREEN BEANS

Preparation Time: 10 minutes

Cooking Time: 15 minutes

Serve: 6

**Ingredients:**

- 1 yellow onion, sliced into rings
- ½ teaspoon onion powder
- 2 tablespoons coconut flour
- 1 and 1/3 pounds fresh green beans, trimmed and chopped
- ½ tablespoon salt

**Directions:**

1. Take a large bowl and mix salt with onion powder and coconut flour
2. Add onion rings
3. Mix well to coat
4. Spread the rings in the baking sheet, lined with parchment paper
5. Drizzled with some oil
6. Bake for 10 minutes at 400 Fahrenheit
7. Parboil the green beans for 3 to 5 minutes in the boiling water
8. Drain it and serve the beans with baked onion rings
9. Serve warm and enjoy!

**Nutritional Value (Amount Per Serving):**

- Calories: 214
- Fat: 19.4g
- Carbohydrates:3.7g
- Protein: 8.3g
- Sugar: 1 g

Preparation Time: 5 minutes

Cooking Time: 5 minutes

Serve: 4

**Ingredients:**

- 1 and ½ tablespoons olive oil
- ¾ pound asparagus, trimmed
- ¼ cup walnuts, chopped
- Salt and pepper to taste

**Directions:**

1. Place a skillet over medium heat, add olive oil and let it heat up
2. Add asparagus; saute for 5 minutes until browned
3. Season with salt and pepper
4. Remove heat
5. Add walnuts and toss
6. Serve warm!

**Nutritional Value (Amount Per Serving):**

- Calories: 124
- Fat: 12g
- Carbohydrates: 2g
- Protein: 3g
- Sugar: 1 g

Preparation Time: 10 minutes

Cooking Time: 25 minutes

Serve: 8

**Ingredients:**

- 1 large cauliflower head
- 2 tablespoons melted coconut oil
- 2 tablespoons fresh thyme
- 1 teaspoon Celtic sea salt
- 1 teaspoon fresh ground pepper
- 1 head roasted garlic
- 2 tablespoons fresh thyme for garnish

**Directions:**

1. Pre-heat your oven to 425 degrees F
2. Rinse cauliflower and trim, core and sliced
3. Lay cauliflower evenly on a rimmed baking tray
4. Drizzle coconut oil evenly over cauliflower, sprinkle thyme leaves
5. Season with a pinch of salt and pepper
6. Squeeze roasted garlic
7. Roast cauliflower until slightly caramelize for about 25 minutes, making sure to turn once
8. Garnish with fresh thyme leaves
9. Enjoy!

**Nutritional Value (Amount Per Serving):**

- Calories: 129
- Fat: 11g
- Carbohydrates: 6g
- Protein: 7g
- Sugar: 2 g

Preparation Time: 10 minutes

Cooking Time: 20 minutes

Serve: 4

**Ingredients:**

- 1 pound fresh green beans, ends trimmed
- 1 and ½ tablespoon olive oil
- ¼ teaspoon salt
- 1 and ½ tablespoons fresh dill, minced
- Juice of 1 lemon
- ¼ cup crushed almonds
- Salt as needed

**Directions:**

1. Pre-heat your oven to 400 degrees F
2. Add in the green beans with your olive oil and also with salt
3. Then spread them in one single layer on a large-sized sheet pan
4. Roast it up for 10 minutes and stir it nicely, then roast for another 8-10 minutes
5. Remove it from the oven and keep stirring in the lemon juice alongside the dill
6. Top it up with crushed almonds and some flak sea salt and serve

**Nutritional Value (Amount Per Serving):**

- Calories: 347
- Fat: 16g
- Carbohydrates: 6g
- Protein: 45g
- Sugar: 2 g

Preparation Time: 5 minutes

Cooking Time: 15 minutes

Serve: 4

**Ingredients:**

- 4 and ½ cups cauliflower, riced
- 3 tablespoons coconut oil
- 1 pound Portobello mushrooms, thinly sliced
- 1 pound white mushrooms, thinly sliced
- 2 shallots, diced
- ¼ cup organic vegetable broth
- Salt and pepper to taste
- 3 tablespoons chives, chopped
- 4 tablespoons butter
- ½ cup parmesan cheese, grated

**Directions:**

1. Use a food processor and pulse cauliflower florets until riced
2. Take a large saucepan and heat up 2 tablespoons oil over medium-high flame
3. Add mushrooms and Saute for 3 minutes until mushrooms are tender
4. Clear saucepan of mushrooms and liquid and keep them on the side
5. Add rest of the 1 tablespoons oil to skillet
6. Toss shallots and cook for 60 seconds
7. Add cauliflower rice, stir for 2 minutes until coated with oil
8. Add broth to riced cauliflower and stir for 5 minutes
9. Remove pot from heat and mix in mushrooms and liquid
10. Add chives, butter, parmesan cheese
11. Season with salt and pepper
12. Serve and enjoy!

**Nutritional Value (Amount Per Serving):**

- Calories: 438
- Fat: 17g
- Carbohydrates: 15g
- Protein: 12g
- Sugar:3 g

Preparation Time: 10 minutes

Cooking Time: 10 minutes

Serve: 4

**Ingredients:**

- 12 cherry tomatoes
- 2 ounces scallions
- 4 portobello mushrooms
- 4 and ¼ ounces butter
- Salt and pepper to taste

**Directions:**

1. Take a large skillet and melt butter over medium heat
2. Add mushrooms and Sauté for 3 minutes
3. Stir in cherry tomatoes and scallions
4. Sauté for 5 minutes
5. Season accordingly
6. Sauté until veggies are tender
7. Enjoy!

**Nutritional Value (Amount Per Serving):**

- Calories: 154
- Fat: 10g
- Carbohydrates: 2g
- Protein: 7g
- Sugar: 0.5 g

Preparation Time: 10 minutes

Cooking Time: No Cook Time

Serve: 6

**Ingredients:**

- ¼ cup crispy chickpeas
- ¼ cup cherry tomatoes halved
- Handful baby spinach
- 2 romaine lettuce leaves, wrapping
- 2 tablespoons lemon juice, fresh
- ¼ cup hummus
- 2 tablespoons kalamata olives, quartered

**Directions:**

1. Take a bowl and mix in all Ingredients: except hummus and lettuce leaves, stir well
2. Put hummus over lettuce leaves, topping with the chickpea mixture
3. Wrap it up and serve
4. Enjoy!

**Nutritional Value (Amount Per Serving):**

- Calories: 55
- Fat: 0g
- Carbohydrates: 12g
- Protein: 3g
- Sugar: 2 g

Preparation Time: 10 minutes

Cooking Time: No Cook Time

Serve: 4

**Ingredients:**

- 1 tablespoon olive oil
- ½ onion, diced
- 10 ounces spinach, chopped
- 12 ounces garbanzo beans
- ½ teaspoon cumin

**Directions:**

1. Take a skillet and add olive oil; let it warm over medium-low heat
2. Add onions, garbanzo and cook for 5 minutes
3. Stir in spinach, cumin, garbanzo beans and season with sunflower seeds
4. Use a spoon to smash gently
5. Cook thoroughly until heated; enjoy!

**Nutritional Value (Amount Per Serving):**

- Calories: 90
- Fat: 4g
- Carbohydrates:11g
- Protein:4g
- Sugar: 3 g

Preparation Time: 10 minutes

Cooking Time: No Cook Time

Serve: 4

**Ingredients**

- 2 avocados, peeled, pitted and diced
- 1 sweet onion, chopped
- 1 green bell pepper, chopped
- 1 large ripe tomato, chopped
- ¼ cup of fresh cilantro, chopped
- ½ a lime, juiced
- Salt and pepper as needed

**Directions:**

1. Take a medium-sized bowl and add onion, bell pepper, tomato, avocados, lime and cilantro
2. Mix well and give it a toss
3. Season with salt and pepper according to your taste
4. Serve and enjoy!

**Nutritional Value (Amount Per Serving):**

- Calories: 126
- Fat: 10g
- Carbohydrates: 10g
- Protein: 2g
- Sugar:43 g

Preparation Time: 5 minutes

Cooking Time: 25 minutes

Serve: 4

**Ingredients:**

- 2 pounds new yellow potatoes, scrubbed and cut into wedges
- 2 tablespoons extra virgin olive oil
- 2 teaspoons fresh rosemary, chopped
- 1 teaspoon garlic powder
- ½ teaspoon freshly ground black pepper and sunflower seeds

**Directions:**

1. Preheat your oven to 400 degrees Fahrenheit
2. Line baking sheet with aluminum foil and set it aside
3. Take a large bowl and add potatoes, olive oil, garlic, rosemary, sea sunflower seeds, and pepper
4. Spread potatoes in a single layer on a baking sheet and bake for 25 minutes
5. Serve and enjoy!

**Nutritional Value (Amount Per Serving):**

- Calories: 225
- Fat: 7g
- Carbohydrates: 37g
- Protein: 5g
- Sugar: 5 g

# DINNER

## PINEAPPLE, PAPAYA, AND MANGO DELIGHT

Preparation Time: 5 minutes

Cooking Time: No Cook Time

Serve: 2

**Ingredients**

- 1-pound fresh pineapple, peeled and cut into chunks
- 1 mango, peeled, pitted and cubed
- 2 papayas, peeled, seeded and cubed
- 3 tablespoons fresh lime juice
- ¼ cup fresh mint leaves, chopped

**Directions:**

1. Take a large bowl and add the listed Ingredients
2. Toss well to coat
3. Put in fridge and let it chill
4. Serve and enjoy!

**Nutritional Value (Amount Per Serving):**

- Calories: 292
- Fat: 11g
- Carbohydrates: 42g
- Protein: 8g
- Sugar: 6 g

Preparation Time: 10 minutes

Cooking Time: 10 minutes

Serve: 4

**Ingredients:**

- 4 Roma tomatoes, diced
- 8 ounces cashew cream
- 2 eggplants
- 1 tablespoon olive oil
- 1 cup parsley, chopped
- 1 cucumber, diced
- Salt and pepper t taste

**Directions:**

1. Slice eggplants into three shtick steaks, drizzle with oil, season with salt and pepper
2. Grill in a pan for 4 minutes per side
3. Top with remaining ingredients
4. Serve and enjoy!

**Nutritional Value (Amount Per Serving):**

- Calories: 86
- Fat: 7g
- Carbohydrates: 12g
- Protein: 8g
- Sugar: 4 g

Preparation Time: 10 minutes
Cooking Time: 15-20 minutes
Serve: 4

**Ingredients:**

- 1 onion, diced
- 1 teaspoon olive oil
- 3 garlic cloves, minced
- 28 ounces tomatoes, canned
- ¼ cup tomato paste
- 14 ounces kidney beans, canned, rinsed and dried
- 2-3 teaspoons chili powder
- ¼ cup cilantro, fresh
- ¼ teaspoons salt

**Directions:**

1. Take a large-sized pot and place it over medium heat, add oil and let it heat up
2. Add onion and garlic, Sauté for 5 minutes
3. Add tomato paste, tomatoes, beans, chili powder and season with salt
4. Lower heat and let it simmer for 10-20 minutes
5. Garnish with cilantro and parsley
6. Enjoy!

**Nutritional Value (Amount Per Serving):**

- Calories: 160
- Fat: 3g
- Carbohydrates: 29g
- Protein: 8g
- Sugar: 7 g

Preparation Time: 5 minutes

Cooking Time: 15 minutes

Serve: 4

**Ingredients:**

- 4 and ½ cups cauliflower, riced
- 3 tablespoons coconut oil
- 1 pound Portobello mushrooms, thinly sliced
- 1 pound white mushrooms, thinly sliced
- 2 shallots, diced
- ¼ cup organic vegetable broth
- Salt and pepper to taste
- 3 tablespoons chives, chopped
- 4 tablespoons almond butter
- ½ cup cashew cream, grated

**Directions:**

1. Use a food processor and pulse cauliflower florets until riced
2. Take a large saucepan and heat up 2 tablespoons oil over medium-high flame
3. Add mushrooms and Saute for 3 minutes until mushrooms are tender
4. Clear saucepan of mushrooms and liquid and keep them on the side
5. Add rest of the 1 tablespoons oil to skillet
6. Toss shallots and cook for 60 seconds
7. Add cauliflower rice, stir for 2 minutes until coated with oil
8. Add broth to riced cauliflower and stir for 5 minutes
9. Remove pot from heat and mix in mushrooms and liquid
10. Add chives, butter, cashew cream
11. Season with salt and pepper
12. Serve and enjoy!

**Nutritional Value (Amount Per Serving):**

- Calories: 438
- Fat: 17g
- Carbohydrates: 15g
- Protein: 12g
- Sugar: 3 g

Preparation Time: 10 minutes

Cooking Time: 10 minutes

Serve: 4

**Ingredients:**

- 12 cups kale, chopped
- 2 tablespoons lemon juice
- 1 tablespoon olive oil
- 1 teaspoon coconut aminos
- Sunflower seeds and pepper as needed

**Directions:**

1. Add a steamer insert to your Saucepan
2. Fill the saucepan with water up to the bottom of the steamer
3. Cover and bring water to boil (medium-high heat)
4. Add kale to the insert and steam for 7-8 minutes
5. Take a large bowl and add lemon juice, olive oil, sunflower seeds, coconut aminos, and pepper
6. Mix well and add the steamed kale to the bowl
7. Toss and serve
8. Enjoy!

**Nutritional Value (Amount Per Serving):**

- Calories: 350
- Fat: 17g
- Carbohydrates: 41g
- Protein: 11g
- Sugar: 7 g

Preparation Time: 5 minutes

Cooking Time: 25 minutes

Serve: 4

**Ingredients:**

- 4 medium zucchinis
- ½ cup marinara sauce
- ¼ red onion, sliced
- ¼ cup kalamata olives, chopped
- ½ cup cherry tomatoes, sliced
- 2 tablespoons fresh basil

**Directions:**

1. Preheat your oven to 400 degrees Fahrenheit
2. Cut the zucchini half-lengthwise and shape them in boats
3. Take a bowl and add tomato sauce; spread 1 layer of sauce on top of each of the boat
4. Top with onion, olives, and tomatoes
5. Bake for 20-25 minutes
6. Top with basil and enjoy!

**Nutritional Value (Amount Per Serving):**

- Calories: 278
- Fat: 20g
- Carbohydrates: 10g
- Protein: 15g
- Sugar: 2.5 g

Preparation Time: 5 minutes

Cooking Time: 5 minutes

Serve: 2

**Ingredients:**

- 1 teaspoon coconut oil
- Pinch of salt
- 1-2 teaspoons nutritional yeast
- 1 small garlic clove, pressed
- 1 slice whole-grain bread

**Directions:**

1. Take a small-sized bowl and add all Ingredients: except bread, mix well
2. Toast your bread with seasoned oil or using a toaster, should take about 5 minutes
3. Once done, spread garlic mix all over toast and serve
4. Enjoy!

**Nutritional Value (Amount Per Serving):**

- Calories: 120
- Fat: 6g
- Carbohydrates: 16g
- Protein: 7g
- Sugar: 4 g

Preparation Time: 15 minutes

Cooking Time: No Cook Time

Serve: 4

**Ingredients:**

- 2 medium English cucumbers, peeled and cut into ¼ inch slices
- 2 tablespoons fresh parsley, chopped
- 3 tablespoons toasted sesame oil
- 2 tablespoons soy sauce
- 1 tablespoon mirin
- 2 teaspoons rice vinegar
- 1 teaspoon brown sugar
- 2 tablespoons toasted sesame seeds

**Directions:**

1. Take a small-sized bowl and add cucumbers, parsley, keep it on the side
2. Take another bowl and add oil, soy sauce, mirin, vinegar, sugar and stir well, pour dressing over cucumbers
3. Let it sit for 10 minutes
4. Spoon cucumber salad into small bowls, sprinkle with sesame seeds and serve
5. Enjoy!

**Nutritional Value (Amount Per Serving):**

- Calories: 108
- Fat: 9g
- Carbohydrates: 6g
- Protein: 1g
- Sugar: 2.5 g

Preparation Time: 5 minutes

Cooking Time: 5 minutes

Serve: 4

**Ingredients:**

- 2 and ¾ cups vegetable stock
- Juice and zest of 1 lemon
- 2 tablespoons fresh thyme, chopped
- ¼ cup fresh parsley, chopped
- Salt and pepper to taste

**Directions:**

1. Take a pot and add the stock, lemon juice, thyme and boil
2. Stir in couscous and cover, remove heat
3. Let it sit for 5 minutes, fluff with a fork
4. Stir in lemon zest and parsley, season with salt and pepper
5. Enjoy!

**Nutritional Value (Amount Per Serving):**

- Calories: 190
- Fat: 16g
- Carbohydrates: 12g
- Protein: 3g
- Sugar: 3 g

Preparation Time: 10 minutes

Cooking Time: 20 minutes

Serve: 6

**Ingredients:**

- 1 large sweet potato, peeled and sliced
- 1-pound Brussels sprouts, trimmed
- 1 tablespoon red wine vinegar
- 2 cloves garlic, minced
- 1/3 cup olive oil
- 1 teaspoon cumin
- ¼ teaspoon salt
- ¼ teaspoon black pepper

**Directions:**

1. Preheat your oven to 400 degrees F
2. Take a bowl and place all ingredients
3. Toss to coat well
4. Take a baking pan and transfer it
5. Lined with aluminum foil
6. Roast for 20 minutes
7. Serve and enjoy!

**Nutritional Value (Amount Per Serving):**

- Calories: 168
- Fat: 12g
- Carbohydrates: 14g
- Protein: 3g
- Sugar: 3 g

# PASTA, SALAD AND SOUP

## WHOLE WHEAT PENNE WITH SUMMER VEGGIES

Preparation Time: 20 minutes

Cooking Time: 5-10 minutes

Serve: 4

**Ingredients:**

- ¾ cups crumbled feta
- ½ teaspoon oregano, dried
- 3 ounces mushrooms, sliced
- 1 and ½ cups cherry tomatoes, halved
- ½ medium yellow pepper, chopped
- 1 medium zucchini, chopped
- 1 and ½ cups fresh broccoli, chopped
- 2 garlic cloves, minced
- 2 teaspoons olive oil
- 6 ounces uncooked whole-wheat penne pasta

**Directions:**

1. Cook pasta according to package instructions, omitting any salt or fat
2. Drain and keep them warm
3. Take a large skillet and place it over medium-high heat, add oil and let it heat up
4. Add garlic, zucchini, pepper and stir well
5. Cook for 2 minutes
6. Add tomato, mushroom, oregano
7. Mix well
8. Lower heat to low, stir for 8 minutes
9. Add veggies with pasta
10. Toss and serve
11. Enjoy!

**Nutritional Value (Amount Per Serving):**

- Calories: 264
- Fat: 7g
- Carbohydrates: 41g
- Protein: 15g
- Sugar: 8 g

Preparation Time: 5 minutes

Cooking Time: 15 minutes

Serve: 6

**Ingredients:**

- 1 tablespoon olive oil
- 1 cup onion, diced
- 12 ounces meatless ground "Beef" flavor crumbles
- 1/3 cup water
- 2 teaspoon Italian seasoning
- 4 cup low sodium veggie broth
- 8 ounces whole-wheat bow-tie pasta
- 2 cup kale, chopped

**Directions:**

1. Take a large skillet and place it over medium-high heat
2. add onion and Saute until tender
3. Stir in veggie crumbles, water, Italian seasoning
4. Cover and cook for 4 minutes
5. Add 2 and ½ cups veggie broth into the mix, bring to ab oil
6. Add pasta and cook accordingly until broth is absorbed for 10-12 minutes
7. Add rest of the broth, chili flakes and kale
8. Cook over 14 minutes more until pasta is done
9. Serve and enjoy!

**Nutritional Value (Amount Per Serving):**

- Calories: 300
- Fat: 7g
- Carbohydrates: 40g
- Protein: 19 g
- Sugar: 5 g

Preparation Time: 10 minutes

Cooking Time: 6 minutes

Serve: 4

**Ingredients:**

- ¾ cup whole wheat noodles, cooked
- 1 teaspoon olive oil
- 1 teaspoon garlic, chopped
- ½ cup spring onions, chopped
- ¼ cup carrots, thinly sliced
- ¼ cup cabbage, shredded
- ¼ cup capsicum, sliced
- ½ cup bean sprout
- Salt as needed

**Directions:**

1. Take a broad non-stick pan and add oil; let the oil heat up over medium heat up
2. Add garlic
3. Add spring onions, carrot, corn, cabbage, capsicum, sprouts and salt
4. Sauté over high-heat for 3-4 minutes
5. Add cooked noodles, sauté for 2 minutes more
6. Serve and enjoy!

**Nutritional Value (Amount Per Serving):**

- Calories: 84
- Fat: 1.8g
- Carbohydrates: 14g
- Protein: 3g
- Sugar: 4 g

Preparation Time: 5 minutes

Cooking Time: 10 minutes

Serve: 5

**Ingredients:**

- 3 and ½ ounces Quinoa
- 3 peaches, diced
- 1 and ½ ounces toasted hazelnuts, chopped
- A handful of mint, chopped
- A handful of parsley, chopped
- 2 tablespoons olive oil
- Zest of 1 lemon
- Juice of 1 lemon

**Directions:**

1. Take a medium-sized saucepan and add quinoa
2. Add 1 and ¼ cups of water and bring it to a boil over medium-high heat
3. Lower down the heat to low and simmer for 20 minutes
4. Drain any excess liquid
5. Add fruits, herbs, Hazelnuts to the quinoa
6. Allow it to cool and season
7. Take a bowl and add olive oil, lemon zest and lemon juice
8. Pour the mixture over the salad and give it a mix
9. Enjoy!

**Nutritional Value (Amount Per Serving):**

- Calories: 148
- Fat: 8g
- Carbohydrates: 16g
- Protein: 5g
- Sugar: 3 g

Preparation Time: 10 minutes

Cooking Time: No Cook Time

Serve: 4

**Ingredients:**

- 4 cups red cabbage, shredded
- 2 cups Napa cabbage, sliced
- 1 cup daikon radish, shredded
- ¼ cup fresh orange juice
- 2 tablespoons Chinese black vinegar
- 1 tablespoon soy sauce
- 1 tablespoon toasted sesame oil
- 1 teaspoon fresh ginger, grated
- ½ teaspoon ground Schezuan peppercorns
- 1 tablespoon black sesame seeds, garnish

**Directions:**

1. Take a large bowl and add red cabbage, napa, daikon and keep it on the side
2. Take a small bowl and add orange juice, vinegar, soy sauce, grapeseed oil, sesame oil, ginger, peppercorns
3. Blend well
4. Pour dressing onto slaw, stir well
5. Taste accordingly
6. Serve and enjoy!

**Nutritional Value (Amount Per Serving):**

- Calories: 95
- Fat: 5g
- Carbohydrates: 12g
- Protein: 1g
- Sugar: 3 g

Preparation Time: 14 minutes

Cooking Time: No Cook Time

Serve: 4

**Ingredients :**

- 2 tablespoons garlic, minced
- 4 cups English cucumbers, peeled and diced
- ½ cup onion, diced
- 1 tablespoon lemon juice
- 1 and ½ cups vegetable broth
- ½ teaspoon salt
- 1 whole avocado, diced
- ¼ teaspoon dried pepper flakes
- ¼ cup parsley, diced
- ½ cup cashew cream

**Directions:**

1. Add the listed ingredients to a blender and emulsify by blending them (except ½ a cup of chopped cucumbers)
2. Blend well until smooth
3. Pour into 4 servings and top with remaining cucumbers
4. Enjoy!

**Nutritional Value (Amount Per Serving):**

- Calories: 169
- Fat: 12g
- Carbohydrates: 9g
- Protein: 4g
- Sugar: 2 g

Preparation Time: 10 minutes

Cooking Time: 10 minutes

Serve: 4

**Ingredients:**

- 3 cups prepared dashi stock
- ¼ cup shiitake mushrooms, sliced
- 1 tablespoon miso paste
- 1 tablespoon coconut aminos
- 1/8 cup cubed soft tofu
- 1 green onion, diced

**Directions:**

1. Take a saucepan and add the stock, bring to a boil
2. Add mushrooms, cook for 4 minutes
3. Take a bowl and add coconut aminos, miso paste and mix well
4. Pour the mixture into stock and let it cook for 6 minutes on a simmer
5. Add diced green onions and enjoy!

**Nutritional Value (Amount Per Serving):**

- Calories: 100
- Fat: 4g
- Carbohydrates: 5g
- Protein: 11
- Sugar: 2 g

Preparation Time: 5 minutes

Cooking Time: 25 minutes

Serve: 4

**Ingredients:**

- 1 tablespoon olive oil
- ½ large onion, diced
- 20 ounces mushrooms, sliced
- 6 garlic cloves, minced
- 2 cups vegetable broth
- 1 cup coconut cream
- ¾ teaspoon sunflower seeds
- ¼ teaspoon black pepper

**Directions:**

1. Take a large-sized pot and place it over medium heat
2. Add onion and mushrooms in olive oil and Sauté for 5 minutes
3. Make sure to keep stirring it from time to time until it browned evenly
4. Add garlic and Sauté for 5 minutes more
5. Add vegetable broth, coconut cream, coconut almond milk, black pepper, and sunflower seeds
6. Bring it to a boil and lower down the temperature to low
7. Simmer for 15 minutes
8. Use an immersion blender to puree the mixture
9. Enjoy!

**Nutritional Value (Amount Per Serving):**

- Calories: 200
- Fat: 17g
- Carbohydrates: 5g
- Protein: 4g
- Sugar: 2 g

Preparation Time: 10 minutes

Cooking Time: 20 minutes

Serve: 3

**Ingredients:**

- 1 cup pumpkin, canned
- 6 cups chicken broth
- 1 cup low-fat coconut almond milk
- 1 teaspoon sage, chopped
- 3 garlic cloves, peeled
- Sunflower seeds and pepper to taste

**Directions:**

1. Take a stockpot and add all the ingredients except coconut almond milk into it.
2. Place stockpot over medium heat.
3. Let it bring it to a boil.
4. Reduce heat to simmer for 20 minutes.
5. Add the coconut almond milk and stir.
6. Serve bacon, and enjoy!

**Nutritional Value (Amount Per Serving):**

- Calories: 145
- Fat: 12g
- Carbohydrates: 8g
- Protein: 6g
- Sugar: 3 g

Preparation Time: 5 minutes

Cooking Time: 25 minutes

Serve: 4

**Ingredients:**

- 1 teaspoon olive oil
- 1 onion, chopped
- 6 garlic cloves, minced
- 1 teaspoon chili powder
- ½ teaspoon ground cinnamon
- ½ teaspoon salt
- 1 can (15 ounces) black beans, drained
- 1 (28 ounces) can, crushed tomatoes, undrained
- 3 cups of water
- 3 celery water, chopped
- 2 cups collard greens, chopped
- 2 tablespoons freshly squeezed lime juice

**Directions:**

1. Take a large soup pot and place it over medium heat, add oil and let it heat up
2. Add onion, garlic and Sauté for 5 minutes
3. Stir in chili powder, cinnamon, salt, beans, tomato with juice, water and bring the mix to a boil
4. Lower heat to low and simmer for 10-15 minutes
5. Use a hand blender to puree the mixture until smooth
6. Stir in greens, cover and let it cook for 10 minutes more
7. Stir in lime juice and serve!

**Nutritional Value (Amount Per Serving):**

- Calories: 200
- Fat: 4g
- Carbohydrates: 30g
- Protein: 12g
- Sugar: 10 g

# VEGETABLE AND SIDE

## TASTY ROASTED BROCCOLI

Preparation Time: 5 minutes

Cooking Time: 20 minutes

Serve: 4

**Ingredients:**

- 4 cups broccoli florets
- 1 tablespoon olive oil
- Salt and pepper to taste

**Directions:**

1. Pre-heat your oven to 400 degrees F
2. Add broccoli in a zip bag alongside oil and shake until coated
3. Add seasoning and shake again
4. Spread broccoli out on the baking sheet, bake for 20 minutes
5. Let it cool and serve
6. Enjoy!

**Nutritional Value (Amount Per Serving):**

- Calories: 62
- Fat: 4g
- Carbohydrates: 4g
- Protein: 4g
- Sugar: 2 g

Preparation Time: 5 minutes

Cooking Time: 12 minutes

Serve: 4

**Ingredients:**

- 2 garlic cloves, minced
- Red pepper flakes to taste
- Salt to taste
- 2 tablespoons coconut butter
- 4 cups green beans, trimmed

**Directions:**

1. Bring a pot of salted water to boil
2. Once the water starts to boil, add beans and cook for 3 minutes
3. Take a bowl of ice water and drain beans, plunge them in the ice water
4. Once cooled, keep them on the side
5. Take a medium skillet and place it over medium heat, add ghee and melt
6. Add red pepper, salt, garlic
7. Cook for 1 minute
8. Add beans and toss until coated well, cook for 3 minutes
9. Serve and enjoy!

**Nutritional Value (Amount Per Serving):**

- Calories: 93
- Fat: 8g
- Carbohydrates: 4g
- Protein: 2g
- Sugar: 1 g

Preparation Time: 10 minutes

Cooking Time: 10 minutes

Serve: 4

**Ingredients:**

- 3 cups carrots, sliced paper-thin rounds
- 2 tablespoons olive oil
- 2 teaspoons ground cumin
- ½ teaspoon smoked paprika
- Pinch of salt

**Directions:**

1. Preheat your oven to 400 degrees Fahrenheit
2. Slice carrot into paper-thin shaped coins using a peeler
3. Place slices in a bowl and toss with oil and spices
4. Layout the slices on a parchment paper-lined baking sheet in a single layer
5. Sprinkle salt
6. Transfer to oven and bake for 8-10 minutes
7. Remove and serve
8. Enjoy!

**Nutritional Value (Amount Per Serving):**

- Calories: 434
- Fat: 35g
- Carbohydrates: 31g
- Protein: 2g
- Sugar: 10 g

Preparation Time: 15 minutes

Cooking Time: 15 minutes

Serve: 4

**Ingredients:**

- 1 pound Brussels sprouts, tough bottom trimmed and halved lengthwise
- 4 shallots, peeled and quartered
- 1 tablespoon extra-virgin olive oil
- Sea salt
- Freshly ground black pepper
- ½ cup roasted pistachios, chopped
- Zest of ½ lemon
- Juice of ½ lemon

**Directions:**

1. Preheat your oven to 400 degrees F
2. Take a baking sheet and line it with aluminum foil
3. Keep it on the side
4. Take a large bowl and add Brussels, shallots and dress them with olive oil
5. Season with salt, pepper and spread veggies on a sheet
6. Bake for 15 minutes until slightly caramelized
7. Remove the oven and transfer to a serving bowl
8. Toss with lemon zest, lemon juice, and pistachios
9. Serve and enjoy!

**Nutritional Value (Amount Per Serving):**

- Calories: 126
- Fat: 7g
- Carbohydrates: 14g
- Protein: 6g
- Sugar: 4 g

Preparation Time: 10 minutes

Cooking Time: 5 minutes

Serve: 4

**Ingredients:**

- 6 small peaches, cored and cut into wedges
- ¼ cup of coconut sugar
- 2 tablespoons almond butter
- ¼ teaspoon almond extract

**Directions:**

1. Take a small pan and add peaches, sugar, butter and almond extract
2. Toss well
3. Cook over medium-high heat for 5 minutes, divide the mix into bowls and serve
4. Enjoy!

**Nutritional Value (Amount Per Serving):**

- Calories: 198
- Fat: 2g
- Carbohydrates: 11g
- Protein: 8g
- Sugar: 3 g

Preparation Time: 10 minutes

Cooking Time: 10-25 minutes

Serve: 4

**Ingredients:**

- 1/2 cup sugar
- 1 mango, sliced
- 14 ounces coconut milk, canned
- 1/2 cup basmati rice

**Directions:**

1. Cook the rice according to package instructions, add half of the sugar while cooking rice. Make sure to substitute half of the required water with coconut milk
2. Take another skillet and boil the remaining coconut milk with sugar; once the mixture is thick, add rice and gently stir
3. Add mango slices and serve
4. Enjoy!

**Nutritional Value (Amount Per Serving):**

- Calories: 550
- Fat: 30g
- Carbohydrates: 70g
- Protein: 6g
- Sugar: 15 g

Preparation Time: 10 minutes

Cooking Time: 20-25 minutes

Serve: 4

**Ingredients:**

- 14 ounces blueberries
- 1 tablespoon lemon juice, fresh
- 1 and ½ teaspoon stevia powder
- 3 tablespoons chia seeds
- 2 cups almond flour, blanched
- ¼ cup pecans, chopped
- 5 tablespoons coconut oil
- 2 tablespoons cinnamon

**Directions:**

1. Take a bowl and mix in blueberries, stevia, chia seeds, lemon juice, and stir
2. Take an iron skillet and place it overheat, add mixture and stir
3. Take a bowl and mix in remaining ingredients, spread mixture over blueberries
4. Preheat your oven to 400 degrees F
5. Transfer baking dish to your oven, bake for 25 minutes
6. Serve and enjoy!

**Nutritional Value (Amount Per Serving):**

- Calories: 380
- Fat: 32g
- Carbohydrates: 20g
- Protein: 10g
- Sugar: 5 g

Preparation Time: 10 minutes

Cooking Time: 15 minutes

Serve: 4

**Ingredients:**

- 1/4 cup applesauce
- 1/2 teaspoon cinnamon
- 1/3 cup raisins
- 1/2 teaspoon vanilla extract, pure
- 1 cup ripe banana, mashed
- 2 cups oatmeal

**Directions:**

1. Preheat your oven to 350 degrees F
2. Take a bowl and mix in everything until you have a gooey mixture
3. Pour batter into ungreased baking sheet drop by drop and flatten them using a tablespoon
4. Transfer to your oven, bake for 15 minutes
5. Serve once ready!

**Nutritional Value (Amount Per Serving):**

- Calories: 80
- Fat: 1g
- Carbohydrates: 16g
- Protein: 2g
- Sugar: 8 g

Preparation Time: 10 minutes

Cooking Time: 15 minutes

Serve: 4

**Ingredients:**

- 2 pounds cherry tomatoes
- 3 tablespoons extra virgin olive oil
- 2 tablespoons balsamic vinegar
- 2 teaspoons garlic, minced
- Pinch of fresh ground black pepper
- ¾ pound whole-wheat linguine pasta
- 1 tablespoon fresh oregano, chopped
- ¼ cup feta cheese, crumbled

**Directions:**

1. Preheat your oven to 350-degree Fahrenheit
2. Line baking sheet with parchment paper and keep it on the side
3. Take a large bowl and add cherry tomatoes, 2 tablespoons olive oil, balsamic vinegar, garlic, pepper and toss
4. Spread tomatoes evenly on a baking sheet and roast for 15 minutes
5. While the tomatoes are roasting, cook the pasta according to package instructions and drain the pasta to a large bowl
6. Toss pasta with 1 tablespoon olive oil
7. Add roasted tomatoes (with juice) and toss
8. Serve with topping of oregano
9. Enjoy!

**Nutritional Value (Amount Per Serving):**

- Calories: 260
- Fat: 15g
- Carbohydrates: 55g
- Protein: 13g
- Sugar: 10 g

Preparation Time: 10 minutes

Cooking Time: 10 minutes

Serve: 4

**Ingredients:**

- 1 cup of coconut oil
- ¼ cup date paste
- 2 tablespoons ground cinnamon
- 4 granny smith apples, peeled and sliced, cored

**Directions:**

1. Take a large-sized skillet and place it over medium heat
2. Add oil and allow the oil to heat up
3. Stir in cinnamon and date paste into the oil
4. Add cut up apples and cook for 5-8 minutes until crispy
5. Serve and enjoy!

**Nutritional Value (Amount Per Serving):**

- Calories: 368
- Fat: 23g
- Carbohydrates: 44g
- Protein: 1g
- Sugar: 14 g

# DESSERT

## QUINOA APPLESAUCE MUFFINS

Preparation Time: 10 minutes

Cooking Time: 15 minutes

Serve: 2

**Ingredients:**

- 2 tablespoons coconut oil
- ¼ cup ground flaxseed
- ½ cup of water
- 2 cups unsweetened apple sauce
- ½ cup brown sugar
- 1 teaspoon apple cider vinegar
- 2 and ½ cups whole wheat flour
- 1 and ½ cups cooked quinoa
- 2 teaspoons baking soda
- Pinch of salt
- ½ cup dried cranberries

**Directions:**

1. Preheat your oven to 400 degrees F
2. Coat muffin tin with liners
3. Take a large-sized bowl and stir in flaxseed, water; add apple sauce, sugar, coconut oil, vinegar, stir well
4. Add flour, quinoa, baking soda, salt, and stir well until just combined
5. Gently fold in cranberries without stirring too much
6. Add 1/3 cup of batter to each muffin tin
7. Bake for 15-20 minutes until top is lightly brown, let them cool for 10 minutes
8. Serve and enjoy!

**Nutritional Value (Amount Per Serving):**

- Calories: 311
- Fat: 17g
- Carbohydrates: 38g
- Protein: 5g
- Sugar: 13 g

Preparation Time: 5 minutes

Cooking Time: 20 minutes

Serve: 6

**Ingredients:**

- 3 cups bran flake cereal
- 1 and ½ cups whole wheat flour
- ½ cup raisins
- 3 teaspoons baking powder
- ½ teaspoon cinnamon, ground
- ½ teaspoon salt
- 1/3 cup brown sugar
- ¾ cup fresh orange juice

**Directions:**

1. Preheat your oven to 400 degrees F
2. Take 12 muffin tins and lightly grease them
3. Add paper liners
4. Take a large bowl and add bran flakes, flour, raisins, baking powder, cinnamon, salt
5. Take another medium-sized bowl and add orange juice, oil, sugar, and mix well
6. Pour wet Ingredients: into dry Ingredients: and mix until moist
7. Fill cups about 2/3rd full
8. Bake until golden brown, should take about 20 minutes
9. Serve and enjoy!

**Nutritional Value (Amount Per Serving):**

- Calories: 222
- Fat: 11g
- Carbohydrates: 32g
- Protein: 6g
- Sugar: 12 g

Preparation Time: 5 minutes

Cooking Time: 20 minutes

Serve: 6 Cups

**Ingredients:**

- 1 cup of water
- 1 cup dried mixed fruit
- 1 teaspoon fresh lemon juice
- ½ teaspoon ground cinnamon
- ¼ cup apple juice

**Directions:**

1. Take a large-sized saucepan and add water, dried fruit, lemon juice, cinnamon
2. Boil over high heat, lower heat and simmer for 20 minutes
3. Remove heat and let it cool for 10 minutes
4. Transfer to food processor and process until smooth
5. Add apple juice and process again
6. Return sauce to saucepan and heat on low heat
7. Serve and enjoy when needed!

**Nutritional Value (Amount Per Serving):**

- Calories: 210
- Fat: 8g
- Carbohydrates: 30g
- Protein: 6g
- Sugar: 12 g

Preparation Time: 5 minutes

Cooking Time: 25 minutes

Serve: 4

**Ingredients:**

- 1 cup apple juice
- ¼ cup of liquid honey
- 4 apples
- ¼ teaspoon ground cloves
- ½ teaspoon nutmeg
- 1 teaspoon cinnamon
- 1 teaspoon fresh ginger root, grated
- 2 dates, pitted and chopped
- ¼ cup dried cranberries
- ½ cup nuts and seeds

**Directions:**

1. Preheat your oven to 325-degree Fahrenheit
2. Take a bowl and add ginger roots, spices, dates, nuts, cranberries, seeds and mix
3. Core apples and stuff each apple with seed and nut mix
4. Drizzle honey
5. Take an 8 x 8-inch square baking dish and add stuffed apples
6. Pour cider around apples
7. Bake for 25 minutes
8. Remove from oven and enjoy
9. Serve!

**Nutritional Value (Amount Per Serving):**

- Calories: 110
- Fat: 15g
- Carbohydrates: 15g
- Protein: 3g
- Sugar: 12 g

Preparation Time: 10 minutes
Cooking Time: No Cook Time
Serve: 12

**Ingredients:**

- 6 cups grated carrot, water removed
- 1 and ½ cups raisins, soaked in water removed
- 1 teaspoon cinnamon, grounded
- 1 cup almonds, soaked overnight and drained
- 1 teaspoon nutmeg, grated
- 1 cup dates, pitted and soaked in water for 1 hour
- 1 lemon zest
- 1 orange zest
- 1 teaspoon cardamom, grounded

**Directions:**

1. Place all Ingredients: in your food processor
2. Pulse until finely ground
3. Take a baking dish and place it firmly
4. Allow setting in the fridge before slicing
5. Serve and enjoy!

**Nutritional Value (Amount Per Serving):**

- Calories: 60
- Fat: 0.3g
- Carbohydrates: 15g
- Protein: 1g
- Sugar: 5 g

Preparation Time: 8 Hours

Cooking Time: No Cook Time

Serve: 2

**Ingredients:**

- 1 cup coconut milk, unsweetened
- 1 medium mango
- 1 tablespoon shredded coconut
- 3 tablespoons chia seeds
- ½ teaspoon vanilla extract
- 1/8 teaspoon turmeric, grounded

**Directions:**

1. Take a bowl and combine coconut milk, vanilla, chia seeds, turmeric into it
2. Whisk until well combined
3. Let it cool in your refrigerator overnight
4. Top with mango and coconut
5. Serve and enjoy!

**Nutritional Value (Amount Per Serving):**

- Calories: 260
- Fat: 9g
- Carbohydrates: 41g
- Protein: 8g
- Sugar: 4 g

Preparation Time: 10 minutes

Cooking Time: 15 minutes

Serve: 6

**Ingredients:**

- ¾ teaspoon pumpkin pie sliced
- 2 apples, cored and sliced
- ½ cup walnuts, chopped
- ½ cup sultana raisins, soaked in water overnight
- 1 tablespoon coconut butter
- 1 orange juice

**Directions:**

1. Preheat the oven to 400 degrees F
2. Take a bowl and add all Ingredients:
3. Toss to combine everything
4. Arrange apples and the rest of the Ingredients: in a baking dish
5. Bake for 15 minutes in your oven
6. Serve and enjoy!

**Nutritional Value (Amount Per Serving):**

- Calories: 93
- Fat: 6g
- Carbohydrates: 9g
- Protein: 2g
- Sugar: 1.5 g

Preparation Time: 60 minutes

Cooking Time: No Cook Time

Serve: 4

**Ingredients:**

- 1 whole medium sweet potato, boiled, then peeled
- 5 tablespoons raw cacao powder
- ¼ cup rice malt syrup
- ¼ cup coconut oil, melted
- 2 cups almond nuts
- A pinch of salt

**Directions:**

1. Take a bowl and mash sweet potatoes into the bowl
2. Add in the rest of the Ingredients:
3. Mix thoroughly until well-combined
4. Take a baking dish and transfer it, then spread evenly
5. Let it cool in the refrigerator
6. Slice them into 12 squares
7. Serve and enjoy!

**Nutritional Value (Amount Per Serving):**

- Calories: 376
- Fat: 32g
- Carbohydrates: 24g
- Protein: 4g
- Sugar: 10 g

Preparation Time: 60 minutes + Chill Time

Cooking Time: No Cook Time

Serve: 10

**Ingredients:**

- 1 cup shredded coconut, dried
- 1 teaspoon vanilla extract
- 1 cup apricot, dried
- 1 cup macadamia nuts, chopped
- 1 cup apricot, chopped
- 1/3 cup turmeric powder

**Directions:**

1. Place all Ingredients: in your food processor
2. Pulse until smooth
3. Pour mixture into a square pan and press evenly
4. Serve chilled and enjoy!

**Nutritional Value (Amount Per Serving):**

- Calories: 201
- Fat: 15g
- Carbohydrates: 17g
- Protein: 3g
- Sugar: 4 g

Preparation Time: 10 minutes

Cooking Time: 15 minutes

Serve: 4

**Ingredients:**

- 2 whole-wheat pitas, cut into wedges
- 2 tablespoons coconut oil, melted
- 1 tablespoon ground cinnamon
- 2 tablespoons brown sugar
- 1 grapefruit, halved
- 2 tablespoons pure maple syrup

**Directions:**

1. Preheat your oven to 375 degrees F
2. Line baking sheet with parchment paper, spread pita wedges in a single layer on baking sheet
3. Brush melted coconut oil
4. Take a small bowl and add cinnamon, brown sugar and sprinkle over pita wedges
5. Bake for 8 minutes
6. Transfer pita to plates
7. Turn oven to broil, place grapefruit halves on a baking sheet, drizzle maple syrup over the top
8. Broil until syrup bubbles for 5 minutes
9. Serve with pita
10. Enjoy!

**Nutritional Value (Amount Per Serving):**

- Calories: 259
- Fat: 28g
- Carbohydrates: 15g
- Protein: 12g
- Sugar: 3 g

Insulin resistance is significantly influenced by dietary habits, which is especially true for physically inactive people. The excessive consumption of high-calorie foods such as fast foods, fatty meats, refined grains, fried foods, and sweetened foods and beverages is believed to be the most significant contributing factor to the rising prevalence of diabetes worldwide, according to research.

As evidenced by the scientific literature, a plant-based diet that is primarily comprised of fruits and vegetables as well as legumes, seeds, nuts, and whole grains is extremely effective in the management of type 2 diabetes and the reduction of comorbidities such as obesity, hypertension, cardiovascular disease, kidney disease, and high cholesterol.

Dietary consumption of animal products is associated with the accumulation of fat in body cells, which interferes with the ability of insulin to perform its normal function of transporting glucose from the bloodstream into cells. It is then possible to develop hyperglycemia and type 2 diabetes due to this increase in glucose levels in the blood. Conversely, fat deposition is reduced, and insulin function can be maintained when eating a plant-based diet containing very little saturated fat. A recent study discovered that the prevalence of type 2 diabetes among vegans is 2.9 percent. In contrast, the prevalence is 7.8 percent among people who primarily consume animal products.

It is believed that hormones released from the small intestine, such as glucagon-like peptide-1 and gastric inhibitory peptide, play an important role in managing overall glucose metabolism and maintaining glucose homeostasis in the body. Therefore, a plant-based diet can help increase the secretion of incretin hormones and improve the function of the pancreatic beta cells, insulin release, and insulin sensitivity, among other things.

In addition to helping people manage their diabetes well, a plant-based diet can lower their risk of developing type 2 diabetes because it contains high levels of antioxidants, micronutrients, fiber, and unsaturated fatty acids, all of which have been shown to have protective effects against the disease. In addition, researchers discovered that the level of glycated hemoglobin (HbA1C), a biomarker that indicates impaired glucose metabolism, remains stable in diabetic patients who adhere to a strict vegetarian diet. Furthermore, a plant-based diet has beneficial effects on various secondary factors associated with diabetes, including physical and emotional distress, quality of life, body weight, total cholesterol, and low-density lipoprotein (LDL) cholesterol, among others.

A plant-based diet combined with regular physical activity helps improve diabetic symptoms. Still, it also helps reduce the need for medications. In addition, plant-based diets are three times more effective at controlling blood glucose levels than conventional diabetic diets, which only restrict calorie and carbohydrate intake.

Interestingly, a plant-based diet high in carbohydrates and fiber results in better control of blood glucose levels and a reduction in total cholesterol and triacylglycerol levels, all of which contribute to a reduction in diabetic complications and improve overall health. In plant-based diets, these effects are primarily due to the inclusion of low-glycemic-index foods (whole grains, fruits, nuts, and legumes) that lower blood sugar levels. In addition, the carbohydrates found in low-glycemic foods are digested, absorbed, and metabolized slower than those found in high-glycemic foods, resulting in a comparatively smaller increase in blood glucose levels. Another advantage of such foods is that they allow large amounts of carbohydrate consumption to replace animal products without the fear of increasing one's glycemic index (GI).

When designing an individualized diet to maximize nutritional health benefits, people with diabetes should consult with their physician or a dietician for guidance. For example, even though not everyone prefers to eat a plant-based diet, small changes in the Diet to increase the proportion of plants and decrease the proportion of animal products can positively impact glucose control and cardiovascular disease risk.

Printed in Poland
by Amazon Fulfillment
Poland Sp. z o.o., Wrocław
23 July 2022

fdc8f8a3-2363-444a-a113-0dfbb1d04971R01